THE BIG IDEA:
OPPENHEIMER & THE BOMB

Paul Strathern was born in London. He has lectured in philosophy and mathematics at Kingston University and is the author of the highly successful series *The Philosophers in 90 minutes*. He has written five novels (*A Season in Abyssinia* won a Somerset Maugham Award) and has also been a travel writer. Paul Strathern previously worked as a freelance journalist, writing for the *Observer, Daily Telegraph* and *Irish Times*. He has one daughter and lives in London.

Oppenheimer & The Bomb

PAUL STRATHERN

ARROW

Published in the United Kingdom in 1998 by
Arrow Books

1 3 5 7 9 10 8 6 4 2

First published in the United Kingdom
in 1998 by Arrow Books

Arrow Books Limited
Random House UK Ltd
20 Vauxhall Bridge Road, London SW1V 2SA

Random House Australia (Pty) Limited
20 Alfred Street, Milsons Point, Sydney,
New South Wales 2061, Australia

Random House New Zealand Limited
18 Poland Road, Glenfield
Auckland 10, New Zealand

Random House South Africa (Pty) Limited
Endulini, 5a Jubilee Road, Parktown 2193, South Africa

Random House UK Limited Reg. No. 954009

A CIP catalogue record for this book
is available from the British Library

Papers used by Random House UK Limited are natural,
recyclable products made from wood grown in sustainable
forests. The manufacturing processes conform to the en-
vironmental regulations of the country of origin

Typeset in Bembo by SX Composing DTP, Rayleigh, Essex
Printed and bound in the United Kingdom by
Cox & Wyman Ltd, Reading, Berks.

ISBN 0 09 923792 X

CONTENTS

INTRODUCTION

Oppenheimer is best remembered today as 'the father of the bomb'. It was he who headed 'the biggest collection of eggheads ever' – who put together the first atomic bomb at the secret laboratories in Los Alamos, in the remote New Mexico mountains. Oppenheimer is also remembered by many as the scientist who was hounded to an early grave by a communist witch-hunt. What is often over-looked is that he also made an original contribution to early quantum mechanics, and published one of the first theoretical models of a black hole.

In between times, Oppenheimer was also a charismatic teacher who inspired a generation of American physicists; and was later director of the Institute for Advanced Study at Princeton for almost 20 years, when giants like Einstein, von Neumann and Gödel were in residence.

Some career, some man. In private Oppenheimer was a slightly odd, highly cultured man. When he saw the first luminous mushroom cloud blooming its false dawn over the desert, he found himself muttering some words from the *Bhagavad-Gita* – a reference which probably escaped the other assembled boffins, generals and intelligence personnel. Oppenheimer was a sophisticated man – but he was a cold fish too. Capable of inspiring great loyalty, he was also regarded by many as élitist and arrogant. This didn't matter so much as long as it was confined to the lab. (Science doesn't develop the personality *per se*, tending to make its practitioners more tolerant of such gaucheness than those in the savage social swim.) But when Oppenheimer became a bigwig in Washington, he quickly made political enemies. It was his arrogance which led to his downfall as much as his left-wing views, no matter how misguided or ambiguous these might have been. 'Oppie', as he was known to his friends, remained a divided man to the end. He was proud to be 'the father of the bomb', but he had no illusions about its horrific potential.

LIFE & THE BOMB

J Robert Oppenheimer was born on April 22nd 1904, in New York City. His father Julius was a German-Jewish immigrant who had made a fortune in the textile importing business. The family home was a luxurious apartment on fashionable Riverside Drive. The Oppenheimers were 'assimilated', having put aside orthodox culture and religion in favour of becoming American plutocrats. Robert's mother Ella was a painter of genuine talent who had studied in Paris. She was strikingly beautiful – apart from a deformed right hand, which she always wore in a chamois leather glove. A family friend described her as 'a very delicate person, highly attenuated emotionally, and she always presided with great delicacy and grace at the table and other events, but a mournful person'. The father was described as 'desperately amiable, anxious to be agreeable, and . . . essentially a very kind man'. But the home had 'a sadness: there was a melancholy tone'.

Young Robert was to inherit a potent blend of these complexities. Indicatively, he grew up (in his own words) 'an abnormally repulsive good little boy.' For the first eight years he was an only child, until a brother called Frank was born in 1912. Robert was educated at the Ethical Cultural School in New York, which believed in instilling high academic standards and liberal ideas – a combination which was then possible in the earnest well-meaning society of the pre-First World War era. At school Robert proved to be a serious-minded, solitary pupil. He quickly asserted both his academic and social superiority, making very few friends in the process. He was tall, with a spindly physique. Somewhat lacking in physical coordination, he soon decided that he didn't like games. (He couldn't stand losing.) But he was no coward, and did possess some physical skills. Typically, he took up solo sailing at the family holiday home on Long Island, and here his daring often bordered on the foolhardy, when he stayed out in squalls. At night he read widely, from minerology to Plato. He particularly liked the aloof melancholy poetry of the modernist T.S. Eliot.

At the age of 18, on a family holiday to Europe, he was struck down with dysentery. It took him a year to recover, during which his teenage rebelliousness made a late appearance. In the words of his mother, this took the form of 'boorishness, and often a complete rejection of my attentions'. The ingrate invalid would lock himself in his room and read.

Eventually the over-intellectual young prig was despatched to a dude ranch in New Mexico to recover. Here he came alive again – as he had only previously done whilst scudding the wind-torn breakers in his yacht. For days he would ride the winding trails through the canyons and over the mountains, camping out at night under the stars.

In 1922, Robert Oppenheimer went to Harvard to study chemistry. A contemporary records: 'I suppose he was lonely, and felt he didn't fit in well with the human environment.' However, in all other environments he was supreme. He still wasn't quite sure what he wanted to do with his life. Besides topping the class at chemistry, he excelled in physics, oriental philosophy, ancient greek and latin, and architecture. Between times he emulated his mother by painting, and even wrote avant-garde poetry which was published in the college literary magazine. All this took time, but as a young man who didn't deign to have a social life and was above such things as a sporting career, Oppenheimer found that he had considerable energies to burn. He was regularly at the labs by 8am, spent the rest of the day attending lectures and working his way through his various subjects in the library, and continued reading into the night. Instead of meals, he would simply break for a hasty 'black and tan': a toasted open sandwich topped with peanut butter and a large dollop of chocolate sauce. This evidently kept his digestive tract sufficiently primed.

Only in his third year did Oppenheimer recognize that his life lay in physics. This was largely due to one man: the physicist Percy Bridgman. An exceptional teacher, Bridgman was to produce the first artificial diamonds under pressure, was later awarded the Nobel Prize, and eventually shot himself. Apart from his temperament, it was Bridgman's understanding of the philosophy of science which interested Oppenheimer. According to Bridgman: 'we do not know the meaning of a concept unless we can specify the operations used in applying the concept in any concrete situations.' Such thinking was profoundly in tune with the latest philosophy of Wittgenstein and the Logical Positivists ('the meaning of a word lies in its verification'). It was also in accord with the continuing rapid advances of quantum theory, which were laying waste the preconceptions of classical physics. Here was a man whose thinking seemed to combine both aspects of Oppenheimer's life – the cultural and the scientific – in a manner that was both intellectually demanding and exciting. It also appealed to the repressed iconoclast in the lanky Lord Fauntleroy of Riverside Drive. As with many exceptional lives, each part made its contribution to the whole. Oppenheimer was never to forget the philosophical questions which Bridgman raised, and their implications for the practice of science. Oppenheimer was hooked: from now on physics was the name of the game, as far as he was concerned.

In 1925, having completed his four-year course in just three years, Oppenheimer graduated from Harvard *summa cum laude*. In those days the Big Science was being done in Europe. Oppenheimer sailed for England and registered at the Cavendish Laboratory in Cambridge, which was then being run by the bluff New Zealander, Ernest Rutherford. Just 15 years previously, Rutherford had rocked the scientific world by proving the existence of the atomic nucleus, founding nuclear physics. By now he had gathered a team of exceptional experimenters who were revolutionizing our understanding of atomic structure.

The 21-year-old Oppenheimer may have been brilliant, but his qualifications hardly impressed Rutherford. In the end Oppenheimer was taken on by the 70-year-old J J Thomson, who had discovered the subatomic particle of negative electricity known as the electron. Oppenheimer was set to work in the laboratory preparing thin films of beryllium (to be bombarded with electrons, so as to investigate their subatomic properties). Oppenheimer was humiliated. Not only was this a mundane task, but he found he couldn't even do it properly. His shortcomings as an experimentalist opened up other deeper uncertainties in his immature buttoned-up personality. 'The lab work is a terrible bore,' he wrote, 'and I am so bad at it that it is impossible to feel that I am learning anything.' These characteristically understated words masked what was in fact a deepening emotional crisis. Oppenheimer had never failed before, *at anything*. Lonely, homesick, and crushed, he fled to Brittany. Here, with the winter wind blowing in his face and the Atlantic waves crashing against the rocks below, he walked the cliffs 'on the point of bumping myself off'. In the end he decided to return to Cambridge and consult a psychiatrist.

Oppenheimer was diagnosed as having incurable *dementia praecox* – the blanket term used by psychiatrists in those days to describe mental illnesses which they didn't understand (now superseded by the term schizophrenia). It was suggested that the patient might benefit from a holiday. Oppenheimer went to Corsica, had a brief holiday romance, and returned with 'a certain improvement in his state of mind'. This was his first relationship, and he never again referred to it except to say that it was 'not a love affair at all, but love'. This facet had evidently been lacking, in any demonstrative form, from his life. Oppenheimer had always been heavily influenced by his mother, but she shared her son's icy temperament, as well as a measure of his arrogant intelligence. For the outwardly superior, but inwardly ever so immature 22-year-old, this first encounter with genuine emotion was something to be savoured and pondered upon in secret.

Oppenheimer had become involved with a psychiatrist, a lover, and a few of the finest scientific minds. There was no doubt which category he saw as the most important, felt closest to, and identified with. But Rutherford, Thomson and Bridgman had all been old enough to be his father. Only now did Oppenheimer encounter an exceptional scientific mind of his own age.

Paul Dirac had been born in England in 1902, two years earlier than Oppenheimer, of an émigré Swiss father and an English mother. Possessing a solitary temperament similar to Oppenheimer's, he preferred to do his work holed up in his rooms above a remote quadrangle at St John's

College. Oppenheimer may have had an exceptional mind, but Dirac was to become one of the greatest theoretical physicists of the 20th century. The two hit it off from the start, though Dirac considered Oppenheimer's vast range of learning to be an unnecessary distraction, if not a complete waste of time. (At the time he met Dirac, Oppenheimer was rapidly adding Italian to his collection of languages, so that he could read Dante in the original.) When Dirac heard that he even *wrote* poetry, he demanded: 'How can you do both – poetry and physics? They are in opposition. In science you want to say something that nobody knew before, in words which everyone can understand. In poetry, it's the exact opposite.' Despite such sentiments, Dirac wasn't above the odd bit of doggerel himself:

'Age is of course a fever chill
That every physicist must fear.
He's better dead than living still
When once he's passed his 30th year.'

And there was some truth in this. Newton's idea of gravity, Einstein's Special Theory of

Relativity, and many other great ideas in physics had been conceived well before their creator's 30th birthday. Dirac was 23, and Oppenheimer was still only 21: they were both young men in a hurry. Already Dirac was working at the cutting edge of quantum theory, which was undergoing an exceptionally complex transformation. The years 1925-6 were amongst the most exciting years in 20th century science. Great, and often seemingly incompatible advances were being made in quantum theory – involving the likes of Bohr, Schrödinger, Heisenberg, Born and anyone bold enough to step into the ring with such heavyweights.

Quantum theory had originated with the German physicist Max Planck in 1900. This accounted for characteristics of electromagnetic radiation (eg, light) which didn't conform with Newtonian mechanics. According to Planck, light was ambiguous: in order to explain its behaviour it had to be regarded as *two different things*. To account for certain effects (such as variations in colour), it had to be regarded as travelling in waves. But in order to explain other phenomena (such as the photoelectric effect, where light bombards a surface and dislodges electrons) it had to be regarded as a stream of particles. These were called photons, and consisted of bundles – or *quanta* – of light.

– But why couldn't light just be regarded as regularly interrupted wavelets of light?
Because in order to dislodge the electrons (in the photoelectric effect) the quanta (photons) had to possess momentum. This requires mass (momentum = mass x velocity).

– But light doesn't weigh anything: so how can these quanta (photons) have mass?
They only have mass when they are in motion. When they are stationary they have zero mass.

– But how can this be? This is yet another impossibility. First light is both waves and particles *at the same time*. Then these quanta are both weightless *and* have mass . . .

Quantum theory was fraught with such ambiguities. For several years attempts were made to patch these up by grafting the principles of quantum theory onto the equations of classical mechanics. But this only led to increasing inconsistencies and paradoxes, especially in the rapidly advancing field of subatomic physics, which was analysing atomic structure. Atoms too seemed to contain wave-particles. Such problems were making it impossible to predict events at this level.

Then in 1925 the wunderkind German physicist Werner Heisenberg, who was only a year older than Dirac, resolved the problem by producing a theory of quantum mechanics. This neatly sidestepped the problem of wave-particle duality by concentrating simply on *observation*. Only the measurable properties of an atom were to be considered as 'real'. The concept of an atom as a minute solar system, containing a sun-like central nucleus (with a positive charge) and orbiting electrons (with negative charge) was abandoned. 'Why speak of an invisible electron path around an invisible atom. If they cannot be seen, they are not meaningful.' Whether whatever was measured was regarded as a wave or a particle didn't matter. The measurements depended upon how they were taken, but the results couldn't disagree with one another. They were simply results.

This was a brilliant insight, but how were such *measurements* to be expressed in a meaningful form without a 'picture' to hang them on (ie, a model, such as the 'solar system' atom)? Heisenberg's work was seen by Max Born, the professor of physics at Göttingen, which along with the Bohr Institute in Copenhagen was the main centre of quantum research. Born suggested that the different measurements could be arranged as rows and columns of numbers in matrix form. Then, by applying matrix theory it would be possible to predict further values for physical variables (such as those applied to particles) and mathematical probabilities for varying energy states (such as those applied to waves). These rectangular rows and columns of figures proved much more useful than a 'picture' of an atom. They gave the first consistent form of quantum mechanics, allowing it to predict in a manner resembling classical mechanics.

This was all far too mathematically complex and theoretical for the famous Austrian physicist and notorious womaniser, Erwin Schrödinger.

Much like Casanova, he wished to *visualize* the naked truth, regardless of physical impediments. Schrödinger remained convinced that it was possible to picture every aspect of the physical universe, even at subatomic level. By the end of 1925, he had produced an alternative version of quantum mechanics. For this he visualized a particle as having a wave associated with it. The properties of such a particle could thus derive from both its particle-like and wave-like nature. Essentially this was a particle which behaved like a wave. Schrödinger then produced a wave equation which could be applied to any physical system (ie, a particle exhibiting wave and particle nature) so long as mathematical values for its energy were known. This form of quantum mechanics became known as 'wave mechanics' to differentiate it from Heisenberg's 'matrix mechanics'.

Heisenberg and Schrödinger soon came to regard one another in much the same fashion as those who hold opposing theories in other fields – from religion to football management. Heisenberg called Schrödinger's theory 'disgusting', while Schrödinger regarded Heisenberg's theory as 'repellent and dispiriting'.

This situation was partially resolved by Oppenheimer's new Cambridge friend Dirac. In mid-1926, Dirac came up with a third theory known as 'quantum algebra'. This demonstrated that matrix and wave mechanics were in fact mathematically equivalent (much to the disgust of their two authors).

Oppenheimer was not in the same class as his friend Dirac and the scientific giants of the German-speaking world. For a start, Oppenheimer's broad educational pursuits had left him insufficiently strong in mathematics. But his physics brain was capable of grasping the most complex concepts – and was indeed raring to do so, after wrestling with the sticky problem of beryllium film. Oppenheimer now began a crash course in the latest quantum advances, at the same time discussing these with Dirac. By May 1926, Oppenheimer had begun to produce a series of papers showing how quantum mechanics resolved a number of complex issues concerning atomic structure. These came to the attention of Max Born, who was so impressed that he invited Oppenheimer to work with him at

Göttingen. Here Oppenheimer was to meet –
and exchange ideas with – the likes of Bohr,
Heisenberg and Fermi. Quantum mechanics was
so new, and developing so quickly, that anyone
who could grasp its complexities and stay abreast
of the latest developments was capable of making
a contribution. Suddenly, Oppenheimer found
himself moving in the big league. He published
joint papers with both Born and Dirac, and
between 1926-9 was to publish no less than 16
papers (including 6 in German) on quantum
physics, making several important contributions.
(The 'Born–Oppenheimer Approximation' re-
mains one of the central notions of quantum
mechanics.) Oppenheimer's major achievement
lay in applying quantum mechanics to the concept of electron spin. (An electron 'spins' on its
axis as it moves around the atomic nucleus, just
as the earth spins to produce night and day as it
orbits the sun.) Electronic spin was to provide the
key to how an atom holds together.

In 1927, Oppenheimer was awarded his PhD
'with distinction' (praise indeed from Göttingen). He then embarked on a tourist trail of
major European research centres, including

Leiden and Utrecht in Holland (at the same time learning Dutch), and meeting up with the great Swiss quantum expert, Wolfgang Pauli, at the Zurich Polytechnic (Einstein's Alma Mater).

By now Oppenheimer knew precisely what he wanted to do with his life. He decided to return to America and devote himself to developing quantum mechanics. He obtained a post as professor of physics at the then little-rated University of California at Berkeley. 'I thought I'd go to Berkeley because it was a desert,' he explained. There was no theoretical physics there, and he would be able to develop his own research as he wished. But just to make sure he wasn't isolated from the latest developments, he also took a part-time job at Caltech in Pasadena, which was already on its way to becoming a world-class scientific research centre. The fact that these two posts were in easygoing California, on the opposite side of America from where he had received his stifling élitist upbringing, was no coincidence. At the ripe old age of 24, Oppenheimer was beginning to loosen up and break free of his background. Indicatively, he now began signing himself J Robert Oppenheimer. The J of course stood for Julius, his father's name – but from now on when he was asked what it stood for, he would reply 'nothing'.

Although Oppenheimer continued with research, his career now effectively entered a second phase – as a teacher. To begin with Oppenheimer had a hopeless teaching manner. Both in lectures and more intimate seminars he mumbled, accompanying his words with ill-at-ease gestures. He would break off, murmuring to himself. But what he had to say was exciting, and it was obvious that he too was excited by his subject. Those who could follow him were soon hanging on his every word. 'Oppie', as he came to be called, quickly achieved cult status. The tall stick-thin figure with the icy blue eyes who chain-smoked and bit his nails, established himself as a charismatic teacher. Not only had he written papers with the likes of Born and Dirac, and discussed quantum theory with Bohr himself, but he also spoke eight languages, read philosophy and wrote avant-garde poetry. Word spread, and in a few years Oppie was attracting brilliant students from far and wide.

These were a mixed bunch. It was now the

1930s: America was in the midst of the Depression and refugees were beginning to flee the deteriorating political situation in Europe, where Hitler now ruled Germany. Typical of Oppie's star pupils were Philip Morrison, who had survived polio and Californian destitution (such as described in Steinbeck's *The Grapes of Wrath*); the 14-year-old prodigy, Rossi Lomanitz, from the wilds of Oklahoma; Hartland Snyder, who had worked as a truck driver in Utah; and later the Jewish-German Bernard Peters, who had escaped from Dachau concentration camp to become a longshoreman in New York before making it out to California. These, and many more, were inspired to become first class physicists by Oppie. As Oppenheimer's students responded to him, he began to discover hitherto unsuspected qualities of leadership. His élitist education had been intended for future leaders of society: Oppie was to the manner born, even if he did smoke in the lecture hall, have rather long hair and wear a blue working shirt. His thinking was equally independent: he led from the front.

But not all were so impressed. Other, more socially perceptive minds detected deep flaws in their scientific star. To them his intense stare and unnervingly awkward manner indicated a man deeply ill at ease with himself. Some regarded him as merely a brilliant dilettante. No man who took such trouble mixing his Martinis 'just so', and casually embarked upon learning sanskrit (as Oppie now did), could be a really serious scientist. He may have been capable of inspired insights, but he couldn't last the distance. Why, he had never written a long paper, or produced any lengthy calculations. Was Oppie just a flash in the pan? Many were offended by his intellectual arrogance: if you couldn't cut the mustard, he simply ignored you. To these he appeared as a cold, calculating, exclusively selfish character, who was constantly playing a role.

So Oppenheimer's late-flowering personality began to develop, with two distinct sides emerging. But who was the *real* Oppenheimer – the brilliant sincere genius, or the arrogant calculating actor? No one could tell: not even Oppenheimer himself, it seemed.

The key appeared to be his need to disguise his emotional insecurity, yet it was this which was now put to the test. In 1936 Oppenheimer fell in love with Jean Tatlock, a psychology graduate student. She had striking dark hair, green eyes and an equally striking personality. The wilful intelligent daughter of a well-known right-wing professor, she had become a member of the Communist Party.

Until now Oppenheimer had expressed the liberal principles of his education, though these had appeared somewhat anachronistic in the light of his social arrogance. The fact is, Oppenheimer maintained precious little contact with the 'real' world. His apartment had no phone or radio, and he never read magazines or newspapers. A colleague recalls that he didn't even know about the 1929 Wall Street Crash until six months later.

With the arrival of Jean Tatlock on the scene, all this changed. Oppenheimer was soon plunged into a life-long involvement in left-wing politics. This transformation can't be entirely attributed to his new love however, as they did in fact first encounter each other at a left-wing meeting called to draw attention to the deteriorating political scene in Europe (which was epitomized by the Spanish Civil War). The fascists were out to get the communists, while the old guard capitalist order turned a blind eye. Left-wing, and even communist allegiances were widespread on the West Coast during this period. There appeared to be no other way of combating social injustice in the America of soup-kitchens, lock-outs and large-scale migrant unemployment.

Oppenheimer had been due for a change. His extracurricular activities (learning sanskrit, reading the *Bhagavad-Gita*) were becoming ever more rarified, and they appeared to be leading nowhere. As indeed was his entire intellectual life. Oppenheimer was belatedly beginning to realize that he would never be a top-flight physicist, like Dirac or Born. To compensate for this he had increasingly busied himself with the intellectual management of his growing band of graduate researchers. Oppie may not have *been* a genius, but it soon became clear that he *had* a genius for organizing high-level research. He seemed to have the knack of getting the best out of the best minds, and knowing how to blend intellectual prima donnas into a working team. An interest in the larger political world was a natural extension of this.

Oppenheimer was growing up rapidly. In all

departments. His crash course in political reality was also accompanied by a crash course in emotional reality. A love affair with Jean Tatlock was a testing experience. She was liable to disappear for days on end, during which Oppie would suffer agonies of jealousy. When she returned she would add fuel to the fire by describing the other men she had been with. Though there are always two sides to such stories, falling in love with an odd fish like Oppie may well have goaded her to such excesses. They became engaged twice, and twice broke it off. A lot of drinking was involved and Oppie's chain-smoking took on a manic intensity. Jean would suffer from crushing depressions, and regularly saw a psychiatrist.

She may have been unstable and demanding, but Jean was the only woman of sufficient emotional force to penetrate Oppenheimer's uncanny reserve. It is significant that just before their relationship became serious Oppenheimer's mother had died of leukaemia. 'I am the loneliest man in the world,' confessed Oppenheimer at the time (though this seems to have been a permanent condition).

In 1937 his father died, leaving him a

considerable fortune. The remnants of the Oppenheimer family now abandoned their patrician East Coast origins. Oppenheimer's younger brother, Frank, had come to study at Caltech, and didn't go back. Frank hero-worshipped his older brother, and was also a highly talented physicist, though not in Oppie's class.

Oppenheimer passed on part of his inherited fortune to fund anti-fascist organizations, unaware that many of these had now become communist fronts. Oppenheimer may have held left-wing views, but he remained a socialist rather than a communist. In the opening stages of his affair with Jean he wavered, but Stalin's treatment of Russian scientists soon made up his mind, irreversibly. It's worth stressing that during this period Oppenheimer had many friends who were communists – amongst whom were several of his research assistants, and also his brother Frank – but he never joined the party himself.

During the summer Oppenheimer would travel to New Mexico. Here he would trek through the mountains on horseback, extending his knowledge of the trails he had first ridden on his earliest trip west when he was 18. Eventually he and his brother acquired a remote hut high amongst the pine woods in the mountains, 80 miles north-east of Sante Fe. Characteristically, Oppenheimer was soon referring to this as his 'ranch' – naming it *Perro Caliente* (Hot Dog), after the expression he had first used on seeing the breathtaking view from its surrounding meadow.

He also travelled further afield, throughout America. His original work on quantum mechanics, and his friendship with the likes of Dirac and Heisenberg, opened many doors. His widespread cultural interests particularly appealed to the émigrés who were arriving from fascist Europe. The cool politeness of his early years was now giving way to a more cultivated charm. At the University of Michigan he discussed radiation with Enrico Fermi, who had recently fled from Mussolini's Italy. Visiting Columbia University in New York he met the Hungarian émigré Leo Szilard, who in 1934 had tried unsuccessfully to patent the nuclear chain reaction which would one day produce the atomic bomb. He also met Einstein and the visiting Bohr at the Institute for Advanced Study

in Princeton. Now that the cream of Jewish–
European scientists had fled such centres as
Göttingen and Berlin, the newly-founded IAS
was rapidly establishing itself as *the* centre for theoretical physics. Oppenheimer knew enough to
be able to converse with the experts, but at the
same time his own original work was not exactly
eclipsed.

Echoing the transformation in his personal life,
his interests had now switched from subatomic
physics to cosmology. Instead of minute atomic
introspection, he had now turned to the universe. In 1939, in conjunction with Hartland
Snyder, Oppenheimer published a paper entitled
'On Continued Gravitational Collapse'. It was
related to Einstein's General Theory of
Relativity, which showed that light was bent
when it passed close to large objects in space.
This meant that space was therefore similarly
bent. (Put simply: nothing can travel faster than
the speed of light – thus if light is curved, then
there is no shorter way between two points
than along this curve.) As part of his General
Theory of Relativity, Einstein produced some
field equations which detailed the relationship

between curved space and the distribution of mass through the universe. These were fiendishly complex, involving no less than 20 simultaneous equations with 10 unknowns.

The solution to these equations produced by Oppenheimer and Snyder showed that when a burnt-out star collapsed under its own gravitational force various odd things happened. Space would be bent in such a tight curve that light emitted from the star's surface would be bent back into the interior of the star. In this way, whatever happened inside the star would be completely sealed off from the rest of the outside universe. A one-way 'event horizon' would be formed. That is to say, particles and radiation would be able to approach the star, yet inside this 'horizon' nothing would be able to come out again. Nothing would be able to escape the tremendous force of its gravity. Instead of the normal dimensions of space, there would be a gap where everything simply vanished. But according to Einstein's Theory of Relativity, time was a dimension of space. This meant that along with space, time would also vanish on the other side of the event horizon. A 'space-time singularity' would result inside this horizon, where infinite gravity compressed everything to finite density. Everything – space, time, particles, radiation – all would disappear as if down an invisible black hole.

This solution to Einstein's field equations flew in the face of all expert cosmological opinion, including that of Einstein himself (who publicly dismissed it as 'ridiculous'). Indeed, the phenomenon was not in fact christened a black hole until the 1960s, when the concept was finally on its way to becoming accepted. Oppenheimer and Snyder were way ahead of their time.

And so they were to remain – yet through no fault of their own. The issue of *The Physical Review* in which Oppie's article appeared was published on September 1st 1939, the day that Hitler invaded Poland and precipitated the Second World War. By a more eerie coincidence, this issue also contained an article by Bohr on the mechanism of nuclear fission, the process which would produce the first atomic bomb – and finally end the war. Though Oppenheimer could have had no idea of it at the time, the subject of Bohr's article was soon to take over his life.

Nuclear fission is essentially the splitting of an atomic nucleus into two roughly equal pieces, a process which releases a vast amount of energy. The theoretical basis of this had been predicted in the first decade of the 20th century by Einstein, as a result of his Special Theory of Relativity. This reaction is encapsulated in his celebrated formula:

$$e = mc^2$$

where e is energy, m is mass, and c is the speed of light. As the speed of light is around three million kilometres per second, it can be seen that a minute amount of mass m releases a stupendous amount of energy e.

For around three decades this remained an entirely theoretical possibility. The situation only changed as a result of experiments conducted with uranium. This element had been discovered over a century earlier by Martin Klaproth, the German pharmacist who founded analytical chemistry. Klaproth's analysis of pitchblende led him to predict that it contained a new element, which he named uranium after the newly discovered planet Uranus. (By an ominous coincidence, this discovery took place in the same year the French Revolution produced European social fission: 1789.) Uranium was duly isolated, and found to have the heaviest known nucleus. It was also found to have a number of isotopes – atoms of the same element which all have the same amount of protons in their nucleus, but have differing amounts of neutrons. These isotopes of uranium were naturally radioactive – in other words they were unstable, and their atomic nuclei were liable to disintegrate spontaneously, emitting alpha particles, electrons or gamma rays.

In the 1930s this instability excited the interest of the German radiochemist Otto Hahn and his Austrian colleague Lise Meitner. They tried bombarding the uranium nucleus with neutrons in the hope of producing some new element which was even heavier than uranium. By 1938, when these experiments had been completed, Meitner had been forced to flee Berlin because she was Jewish. But her long-term professional partner Hahn, who had helped her to flee, kept her posted of the results. These had not been successful: no heavier element had been produced.

Instead the results had thrown up a seeming impossibility. The uranium bombarded with neutrons seemed to have produced barium, an element which was around half the weight of uranium.

It was Meitner who realised what had happened. The uranium nucleus had split in two. She named this process nuclear fission. Meitner realised that besides the production of barium, a great deal of energy which had previously bound the nucleus together was also released. She was able to calculate that *each single atomic nucleus* of uranium had released a massive *2000 million* electron volts of energy.

Bohr had outlined the theoretical mechanism of nuclear fission. Hahn and Meitner had shown how it could be achieved. When Bohr learned this news, he realized at once its sensational implications. This process could be used to produce an explosion the like of which had never been seen, or even dreamt of, before. And this process was known in Nazi Germany.

Bohr learned this news just before the outbreak of the Second World War in 1939. At the time, he had left his native Denmark and was on a lecture tour of the United States. Horrified at these developments, the anti-Nazi Bohr immediately contacted Einstein in Princeton. He warned Einstein of the disastrous possibilities now arising from his famous formula. Einstein discussed the matter with Szilard, and the two of them secretly wrote a letter to President Roosevelt, warning him of the situation.

After rapid consultations with military and scientific experts, Roosevelt inaugurated a project to build an American atomic bomb, before one was built by the Nazis. In an ironic, but typical development, Einstein was not informed of the top secret Manhattan Project, as it came to be known. The 'intelligence' services deemed that the man who had actually informed them of the danger was too much of a security risk to be allowed to know what was going on. This was to be just the first move in an ongoing tragi-farce which was to ruin many innocent lives, whilst leaving genuine spies to go about their business unmolested. It is difficult to exaggerate the level of this absurdity. One fact will have to suffice. At this time (and for almost *fifty* years: 1924-72) the FBI was run by a paranoid drag queen who was being blackmailed by the Mafia, and himself later blackmailed presidents to keep his job. This was of course J Edgar Hoover.

Meanwhile in the similarly wondrous world of nuclear physics, Szilard contacted his colleague Fermi and together they set about working out the practicalities of large-scale nuclear fission. Szilard had already done important work in this field, having shown that when the uranium nucleus was struck by a neutron, and split, it released on average two or three neutrons (along with the large quantity of energy). Szilard had understood the significance of this. If uranium nuclei could be contained so that the released neutrons did not escape, but went on to split further nuclei, which then released further neutrons, which went on to split even more nuclei . . . a self-perpetrating chain reaction would start, releasing gargantuan amounts of energy.

But all this was by no means as simple as it sounded. Bohr had already suggested that when nuclear fission took place in uranium, it would in fact only involve the isotope uranium-235 (the figure refers to its atomic weight). This isotope made up a mere 1 part in 140 of natural uranium.

The main constituent, uranium-238, would for the most part just absorb the bombarding neutrons.

In 1941 Fermi built a nuclear reactor in a squash court at the University of Chicago. Fermi's first experiments quickly confirmed Bohr's prediction that under normal circumstances no chain reaction would take place with natural uranium. A way had to be found to ensure that the free neutrons managed to react with the uranium-235.

Fermi found himself faced with a formidable series of related problems. What was the necessary mass of uranium required to bring about a chain reaction? What was the best means of using the released neutrons and ensuring they didn't escape? How could the reaction be controlled? When the uranium-235 nucleus split, the two or three free neutrons which it released were 'fast' neutrons of high energy which were easily absorbed by uranium-238. These fast neutrons somehow had to be slowed down, so that they could continue splitting the rarer uranium-235 nuclei.

Fermi eventually solved this problem by

inserting large quantities of graphite rods into the natural uranium. When the fast free neutrons collided with the light moderator atoms of graphite, they would slow down, enabling them to make contact with the uranium-235. This enabled the chain reaction to continue, in a controlled manner. However, if the carbon rods were not inserted in the uranium pile in precisely the right manner, an uncontrolled nuclear explosion was liable to result. This could have proved lethal for the surrounding blocks, and devastated a large area of the city. Fortunately for the unsuspecting citizens of Chicago, Fermi was pretty certain he knew what he was doing. Fingers crossed, and on December 2nd 1942 the world's first nuclear reactor produced the first controlled, self-sustaining nuclear reaction.

Had Chicago been devastated, the intelligence services might have had some explaining to do. Fermi was still an Italian citizen, and at the time the United States was at war with Italy. (The excluded Einstein had, of course, been a US citizen for several years.)

To achieve efficient nuclear fission on a large scale, it was necessary to concentrate the

fissionable U-235 above the low 1 in 140 pro-
portion in which it occurred naturally. Unfortunately this couldn't be done by any chemical
process, as the chemical properties of the isotopes
were virtually indistinguishable. This meant they
would have to be separated physically – in other
words, separated according to the atomic size of
the different isotopes. Some task. At atomic level
the difference in size between the two isotopes
was minute. Nevertheless, various projects were
set up to investigate this problem.

At the Westinghouse Research Laboratory in
Pittsburgh they began trying to separate the
heavier U-238 from U-235 by centrifugal force.
Ingenious, but it proved ineffectual. At
Columbia University in New York, a gaseous
diffusion process was attempted. This involved
forcing the uranium in gas form through a very
fine porous barrier. The smaller isotope U-235
would pass through more quickly, and the first
amounts gathered on the other side would thus
contain a higher concentration of U-235. This
process could be repeated, constantly enriching
the uranium, until almost pure U-235 was
obtained.

Sounds simple enough, but as always the problems were formidable. Far from being a gas, uranium is in fact a very hard and heavy metal. To prepare the uranium for the gaseous diffusion process it therefore had to be converted into uranium fluoride, which is a gas. The snag here was that uranium fluoride proved so violently corrosive that nothing could hold it. No container had yet been made that could contain this gas. And the same inevitably applied to any diffusion barrier to be used in the process, let alone any pipes, taps or pumps required to hold and transmit and control the gas.

Some problems, some solutions. In order to overcome these problems, a new industry was born. First the chemists had to come up with a brand new chemical plant designed with entirely new materials, and then the manufacturing process would have to begin in earnest. Two vast secret sites were selected for the gaseous diffusion plants – one at Hanford, occupying a desolate valley along the Columbia River in Washington State, and another covering 52,000 acres at remote Oak Ridge in Tennessee (where Oppenheimer's brother Frank was employed).

The scale of these projects was stupendous. A few figures will give an idea. Almost 45,000 construction workers were employed at the Hanford site, and the plant erected at Oak Ridge was the largest building in the world (like a vast slab skyscraper laid on its back). Besides Frank Oppenheimer, 25,000 technicians were set to work in this building. America was in earnest. At the beginning of the Manhattan Project, the government earmarked a preliminary $6,000 for the project. The final cost was to be over $2 billion. (Quite a sum, when many of the construction workers were receiving less than $3 a day.) Such a concentration of manpower and technical ability had never previously been assembled throughout history. (Similar manpower had been employed on the pyramids, and in the 20th century on digging the White Sea Canal in Soviet Russia, but in both cases almost all those employed were unskilled slaves, and treated as such.) By the end of the war the Manhattan Project was larger than the entire US automobile industry.

But this was just preparation work – providing the necessary material. For all this to be of any use, someone had to work out how to make it into a bomb. Here were *scientific* problems on a scale never before encountered. For this task, it would be necessary to assemble the best scientific brains in the country (minus Einstein, of course). And these brains would have to be controlled so that they worked together as a team.

Who was of sufficient scientific calibre and status to direct such a project? Who knew the best scientific brains in America, knew how to inspire and direct teams of first-rate young scientists? Who was abreast of all the latest developments in nuclear physics? One man had all these qualifications: J Robert Oppenheimer.

The overall command of the Manhattan Project had by now passed into military hands – specifically the large beefy hands of General Leslie R Groves. As an energetic military engineer, Colonel Groves had recently built the Pentagon. Promotion and physical expansion had followed – producing a 17-stone general. No one wanted to spend the war looking after a bunch of goddamn scientists, so Groves was given the job of running the Manhattan Project. Further promotion and expansion followed. In the words of one of his colleagues: 'He's the biggest sonovabitch I've ever met in my life, but also one of the most capable individuals.' Yes, General Groves was big, and General Groves was a bastard. 'I hated his guts and so did everyone else,' added his military pal. Groves may have been a very big man, but he now had a very big job on his hands – especially for someone whose postgraduate know-how had largely been confined to large construction sites.

Groves and Oppenheimer were chalk and cheese. But to the surprise of those concerned the spindly aloof physicist and the big brash general hit it off. Right from the start they understood each other. Which was very lucky for those concerned – Groves didn't *have* to choose Oppenheimer. The decision was entirely his, and it was inspired.

Oppenheimer immediately suggested that the development of the bomb itself should be concentrated in a single location. This would include all chemical and metallurgical research, all nuclear physics (both theoretical and practical), and preliminary detonation experiments. It would be the top secret site where they would actually create the bomb.

But where to put it? Oppenheimer knew just the place. He took Groves up into the mountains of New Mexico, 35 miles north-west of Santa Fe. Here he showed him the site of an old Indian school on a plateau – miles from the nearest habitation, with views through the clear mountain air to the distant snow-capped peaks of the sierras. Groves was suitably impressed: you couldn't get much more secret than this. So Oppenheimer fulfilled the dream of a lifetime – to combine his two obsessions: science and mountains. The name of the Indian school was Los Alamos (The Poplar Trees).

Los Alamos was 7,000 feet up, at the end of a donkey trail. The nearest contact with civilization was a desert whistle-stop on the railway line from Santa Fe to nowhere. When you got off the train, it was like the set of *High Noon*. There was nothing, and nobody, for as far as the eye could see in all directions. Such was the encouraging sight which greeted the 3,000 construction workers drafted in to build the road up through the mountains, linking Los Alamos with the outside world. The site itself became a hive of industry, with groups of low buildings and rows of huts erected along open avenues, military style. Groves supervised construction in the tight-fisted fashion the army had come to appreciate. (He'd brought in the Pentagon well under budget. But when the inmates of this new building were confronted with the bills for Groves' gaseous diffusion plants at Hanford and Oak Ridge, they began to wonder if there'd be anything left to run the war. Groves was given a firm dressing down, and issued with strict instructions to cut down on 'everything except the bomb itself'.)

The growing town in the wilderness would eventually accommodate 3,000 – with some of America's brightest young scientists finding themselves crammed into tin huts designed as punishment corps' barracks. Such luxuries as pavements and streetlights were dispensed with, in this centre of modern technology. Air conditioning and heating were not initially considered necessary – until the baking desert dustbowl of summer gave way to the frigid quagmire of winter. Even so, water remained in such short supply that it had to be piped in. (During winter the pipeline often froze solid, but Groves had 'economized' on water tankers.)

Oppenheimer now set about trying to persuade the finest scientists in America to live and work there. This would not have been easy at the best of times – but Oppenheimer found himself hampered by some unusual difficulties. He wasn't allowed to inform his recruits where they were going. He couldn't tell them how long they'd be there (no one knew that). And he was absolutely forbidden to tell them what they would be doing. But Oppenheimer evidently possessed cunning powers of persuasion. According to one recruit: 'It was romantic . . . Everything was clothed in the deepest secrecy. We were all to join the army and then disappear to a mountain-top laboratory in New Mexico.' (From the sound of it, Oppie couldn't refrain from letting drop the beauties of his beloved New Mexico.) The names of those recruited to work at Los Alamos reads like a who's who of top physicists – of Oppenheimer's period, and the great post-war generation to follow. Fermi and von Neumann are perhaps the best-known of the older generation. Younger recruits included the 24-year-old Richard Feynman, the practical joker who was to become one of the finest minds in physics; and as part of the contingent recruited from England came Richard Wilkins, who later received the Nobel Prize for his work on the discovery of DNA. Actual and future Nobel laureates were thick on the ground. It was General Groves, in customary fashion, who described this as 'the biggest collection of eggheads ever'. And he was right. Not even at the Cavendish Laboratory in Cambridge, at Göttingen or Berlin, or even at the Institute for Advanced Study in Princeton, had there ever been such a concentration of genius. Nor has there been since (which is fortunate, when one considers what they were up to). However, not everyone was so impressed by Oppenheimer's offer. Szilard, who knew enough of what was going on to be told details of the remote location, protested: 'Everyone who goes there will go crazy.'

Oppenheimer was obviously the perfect choice to direct the project at Los Alamos. Or was he? Doubts soon began to be expressed. Oppenheimer had no real administrative experience whatsoever. All he had ever directed were a few small teams of physicists at Berkeley. He may have had a razor-sharp mind, and he may have been capable of lightning insights which left brilliant minds standing, but there was still the nagging problem about the depth and persistence of his work. Oppenheimer was an intellectual sprinter: he'd never undertaken a big long-term project before. (And what could be bigger than this one?) Then there was the question of his experimental abilities. The practical ineptitude he had shown in the labs at Cambridge had by now grown to legendary proportions. (His nickname 'Buster' Oppie referred to Keaton-like episodes as well as lab bills.) And on occasions even his theoretical work fell into this category. His assistants learned to look out for *Oppenheimer factors*: missing mathematical signs and symbols in his calculations.

All this quickly became common knowledge in a breeding ground of gossip such as Los Alamos. Yet no other man at Los Alamos had such a grasp of the basic questions of particle physics and nuclear fission. He knew what he was talking about with *everyone* – with the possible exception of General Groves.

Yet ironically it was General Groves who had supported Oppenheimer against the Washington experts who questioned his professional abilities. ('Oppenheimer is a *bona fide* genius who knows what he's talking about.') But worse was to come. Whether or not Oppenheimer was up to the job was irrelevant – in the eyes of the intelligence services. Groves now began receiving alarming security reports about Oppenheimer from California. Oppenheimer was a communist spy. His girlfriend was a member of the Communist Party, and so was his brother Frank. (Though oddly this had not prevented Frank from getting a senior job at the top secret Oak Ridge uranium processing plant.) Groves confronted Oppenheimer with the security reports and demanded an explanation. The hard-headed general was deeply impressed by the frankness and convictions of his favourite genius. The West Coast security chiefs were asked to desist (or words to that effect).

Oppenheimer was now 38 years old, and his life had undergone another transformation. At least, so it appeared. During one of the off periods of his hectic on-off relationship with Jean Tatlock, Oppenheimer had met 33-year-old Kitty Harrison, a naturalized American who had been born a German princess. They fell in love at once. Not surprisingly, Mr Harrison was none too pleased at this development. But Kitty was adept at getting divorces (she'd already had two), and within months she'd married her fourth husband – to become the first Mrs Oppenheimer. The following year, 1941, a son was born.

Oppenheimer took to family life and settled down somewhat. He now preferred to stay at home rather than attend political meetings, as did Kitty, who shared his left-wing sympathies. By mid-1943 the family had moved to Los Alamos. But every few months Oppenheimer had to return to Berkeley to supervise the removal of equipment and further recruiting. On these trips he was always dutifully trailed by the FBI. Occasionally he would meet Jean Tatlock, who was becoming increasingly unstable and desperate for support. On more than one occasion this resulted in him staying overnight at her apartment. We will never know what happened on these occasions – and maybe it's none of our business. Though we can always try and imagine. Just like the FBI did – in suitably lurid fashion. Los Alamos was duly informed that Oppenheimer should be 'completely removed from the project and dismissed from employment by the United States government'. The clean-living FBI would tolerate neither communists nor adulterers: the unmarried J Edgar Hoover was insistent upon this point.

But this was more than just a farce. In 1944, Jean Tatlock committed suicide. The FBI of course knew at once, but amidst the heat of their investigations the news of her death was not passed on to Oppenheimer for over a month. After receiving the news Oppenheimer silently left the laboratory and disappeared into the surrounding pine forest for several hours. Home life in the isolation of Los Alamos was not going smoothly. Kitty had returned to the heavy-drinking ways which had already seen her through three marriages. In the evenings when he wasn't working, Oppenheimer continued mixing his Martinis, icy as ever. Such was the personal life of the man who presided over what was to become humanity's greatest collective intellectual achievement. (Though what the object of this achievement says about the psychology of humanity is another matter. It is surely no accident that having discovered how to destroy its planet, humanity's next great collective intellectual achievement was directed towards escaping from it.)

The assembled geniuses at Los Alamos were now faced with a task of fiendish technical complexity. How were they to convert the chain reaction nuclear fission, which Fermi had produced in Chicago, into a viable weapon? Or in simple military terms, such as those employed by General Groves: how to make it into a bomb you could actually drop on someone.

The first problem to be solved was the amount of uranium needed. Below a certain weight (known as the critical mass) U-235 does not achieve chain reaction nuclear fission. In this state the neutrons released by the split nuclei usually scatter before they can strike another nucleus. As the mass of U-235 is increased, so the likelihood of the chain reaction occurring increases. Above a certain critical mass, a neutron released by the initial fission will on average strike another nucleus, splitting it. The released neutrons in turn split further nuclei, in a rapidly multiplying chain reaction. All this takes place at vast speed, in an uncontrollable reaction, releasing a vast amount of energy, and an atomic explosion is produced.

It was apparent that any atomic bomb would have to contain two subcritical masses of uranium, which could then be brought together. Hey presto! Inevitably, things didn't work out quite as simply as that. For a start, the fissionable material had to be brought together to form a critical mass at tremendous speed – or the uncontrollable chain reaction simply wouldn't take place.

To overcome this problem a 'gun' detonator was evolved. This gun-type bomb became known as 'Little Boy'.

The explosive is detonated, firing the uranium bullet. When this reaches the uranium target, the critical mass is exceeded and a nuclear explosion takes place.

Unfortunately, it soon became apparent that even this method had its snag. Although the two subcritical masses of uranium came together almost simultaneously, there was still a danger

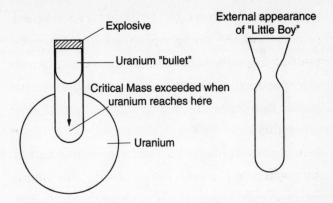

from the stray neutrons emanating from the uranium before the critical mass was achieved. These were liable to cause a much smaller premature explosion, which would take place before the material could fully explode. The effect of the bomb would then be immeasurably lessened.

This problem was foreseen during the meticulous theoretical work conducted by the physicists at Los Alamos. It was up to them to produce a solution, which they did. If the U-235 bullet was fired fast enough, it appeared that the problem wouldn't arise. But how fast would the bullet have to be fired? According to the most precise calculations possible, it would need to travel at 1,000 metres per second. Unfortunately, the US Army had no gun capable of firing at such a speed. Oppenheimer and his team set about the difficult task of designing an appropriate gun, which could also fit into 'Little Boy'.

In the early summer of 1943, a bright young spark from the ordnance team approached Oppenheimer with an alternative idea. Seth Neddermeyer suggested that instead of using a bullet to bring about critical mass, this could more simply be achieved by using the mass that was already there, and *concentrating* it until it reached the *density* required for the explosion to take place. This could be done by an implosion. A metal pipe could be filled with uranium, which could be surrounded by explosive and encased in a larger pipe. When the explosive was detonated, this would implode the pipe, instantaneously concentrating the uranium to critical density and . . . hey presto!

Unfortunately, the difficulty here was that the pipe had to be collapsed evenly, otherwise parts of the uranium would implode prematurely, thus preventing the full nuclear blast. Von Neumann calculated that if the implosion was to be successful the variation in the symmetry of the shock wave could not exceed 5%.

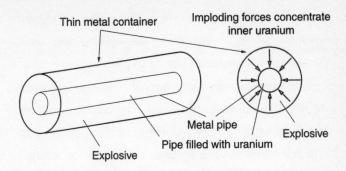

Oppenheimer was impressed by Neddermeyer's ingenious approach, judging that he had 'originality and a fine mind'. The assembled geniuses working on the 'bullet' method were less impressed. No matter how heavily the pipe was stopped up, the explosive effect would surely just cause the uranium to squeeze out of the ends. If it was to be done this way, why not encase the uranium in a *sphere* of packed explosive?

Neddermeyer dismissed this out of hand. In his view the technical difficulties of achieving an even detonation in a sphere were all but insurmountable. Besides, it would be impossible to conduct experiments to discover if the implosion *had* been evenly distributed – this was only possible with a pipe, which you could examine *after* it had been subjected to an experimental explosion. Oppenheimer saw the point. Nedder-meyer and his team were dispatched into the desert with a large supply of explosives.

Throughout the summer of 1943 a series of daily explosions boomed and echoed through the canyons around Los Alamos, as Neddermeyer and his team sought to blast their way to a suit-able answer. Yet no matter how they set the explosions, the imploded pipe always ended up twisted, indicating that the explosive force had not been even. Then the ingenious Nedder-meyer realized that the solution to his problem was the same as that required for the bullet method. Speed! And to achieve a greater speed of implosion he didn't need to manufacture any special high-powered gun: all he needed was greater explosive power.

Bigger bangs began echoing around the hills. But unfortunately this method of experimenting soon proved to be self-defeating. Above a certain level of explosive power, the pipe was simply destroyed – blown up! This meant there was no evidence to check whether the implosion had in fact taken place evenly, or not. And Oppen-heimer was adamant that there should be nothing whatsoever left to chance with the 'gadget' – as they began calling the bomb up at Los Alamos. The 'gadget', 'Little Boy', and later 'Fat Man' – for the implosion bomb. In retrospect such names appear particularly telling: how innocent it all sounded! Those who worked at Los Alamos claim the pressure was such that there was no time to think about what they were *actually* doing. Even those who were later to have their doubts about the effect of the bomb, and its consequences on world history, only articulated these worries during the later stages, and then only amongst themselves. The enormity of what they were doing had not yet dawned on them.

Meanwhile, the programme for producing the bomb's ingredients continued apace. Fat Man required a massive diet. The production problems, and their solutions, remained on a gargantuan scale. The gaseous diffusion process, by which the natural uranium was enriched to higher concentrations of U-235, required huge quantities of corrosive uranium fluoride gas to be sucked through a porous barrier. Yet it took tons of uranium (which then had to be turned into gas) merely to produce less than a teaspoonful of

U–235 (and even this was only 15% pure). The plant at Oak Ridge, housed in its toppled and flattened Empire State building, required the largest vacuum system ever conceived. It needed more power to keep it going than Pittsburg, and its copper requirements quickly exhausted the entire US copper reserves. To make good this shortfall, 6000 tons of silver ingots from the US reserves were despatched from Fort Knox, and reduced to wire. (This was to be returned after the war, minus the natural 'evaporation' that takes place whenever silver is handled by skilled operators.) The magnets on which this silver wiring was used weighed up to 10,000 tons, and were so powerful that the plant workers could feel them pulling the nails of their boots. All this, to produce a coffee bean of fissionable material. Even on this scale, it just wasn't enough.

Nor would it have been, but for an important discovery by Fermi. During his experiments with the world's first nuclear reactor in Chicago, Fermi had produced small quantities of the newly-discovered element plutonium, in the form of its radioactive isotope P–239. This was a major advance, for P–239 had a critical mass which was only *one third* that of U–235. Even more useful, P–239 was produced in nuclear reactors when neutrons bombarded the large quantities of unfissionable U–238 left over after U–235 was extracted.

Here was another fissionable material that could be used in an atomic bomb. The massive plants at Oak Ridge and Hanford now began producing plutonium as well. But this was much more than just a 'brute force' manufacturing operation producing minuscule amounts of useable material. Aside from requiring immense skill (on a grand scale), it also required even greater care (on an even grander scale). Fissionable plutonium is a deadly radiological killer, owing to its high-rate emission of alpha particles – which are absorbed straight into the bone marrow and cause leukaemia. Any amount above 0.13 milligrams is deadly to a human being (a speck of dust could account for an entire hut of workers, and did).

Despite the massive input, and the addition of plutonium, production of fissionable material remained pitifully small through 1943. The massive unwieldy dynamos at Oak Ridge were liable to break down for weeks on end, and as if this wasn't enough, even greater impetus was given to the Manhattan Project by the news Niels Bohr now brought to America.

In 1943 Bohr finally managed to flee German-occupied Denmark; from neutral Sweden he was secretly flown across the North Sea to Britain. Bohr arrived at Los Alamos along with a batch of British nuclear scientists who had been flown over to aid the project. He also brought with him some alarming information. Shortly before he'd fled, Bohr had been visited by Heisenberg, one of the few top scientists who had remained behind in his native Germany. Bohr asked him if the Germans were attempting to make an atomic bomb. Heisenberg had been equivocal, causing Bohr to understand that they were at an advanced stage. As soon as he arrived at Los Alamos, Bohr passed on this news to Oppenheimer.

Oppenheimer knew there was no time to lose. But he was also intimately aware of every detail of what was going on at Los Alamos: the technical problems were still insurmountable. On top of this, he was hardly being helped by Los

Alamos 'intelligence'. They too had now worked out that Oppenheimer knew everything that was going on – and they had also worked out that he was definitely a communist spy. Wherever he went, Oppenheimer was accompanied by a group of 'minders', ostensibly for his own security. Meanwhile, amongst the batch of new British arrivals was the nuclear scientist Klaus Fuchs, who quickly established contact with a like-minded friend. Regularly he would drive down to Santa Fe and pass on the latest details of America's atomic bomb project – which speedily winged their way to Russia.

Running the team of dedicated top scientists at Los Alamos was much like running a team of highly skilled people in any other field, from opera to a rugger scrum. Each person knew the certain way to achieve success – his way. Likewise, there was only one answer to every problem, and each person knew what that was. Scientists are seldom reticent, especially when they are the best and are working in their own field (a qualification which often applied to all present at meetings in Los Alamos). Oppenheimer knew enough in all the relevant fields to command respect, and knew enough to shut up during the screaming matches. Afterwards he would privately smooth the ruffled feathers, explaining what he had decided. Few were ever fired, and those moved sideways would continue to contribute – their new perspective often adding a crucial dimension. Oppie proved himself an extremely able politician in every department (except his politics, which were ignored by all but his dogged retinue).

Yet certain problems remained intractable. Oppenheimer's faith in Neddermeyer and his implosion method was tested to the limit. By early 1944, tracts of the countryside around Los Alamos were beginning to look as if they had already been devastated by an atomic blast. Yet all to no avail. The next failed explosion took everyone by surprise, especially Neddermeyer. For the first time Oppie blew a fuse. Neddermeyer was bawled out, banished to one of the more obscure Los Alamos labs, and forbidden to detonate anything so much as a match. Implosion was out!

No sooner had Oppenheimer calmed down than he found he had to eat his words. It was discovered that plutonium emitted a large amount of 'stray' neutrons. These were bound to set off premature fission if the 'bullet' method was used. So a way *had* to be found to make the implosion method work. Grimly, Oppenheimer conceded the case and ordered the implosion team back to work. Minus Neddermeyer (there were limits).

With their single-minded leader out of the way, the implosion team was now free to experiment with the spherical approach. But how was the explosive to be assembled, so as to ensure an even detonation? Such supreme young physicists as Feynman, and old maestros of the calibre of the great von Neumann, now turned their brains into computers as they struggled to work out the answers. What were the mathematics which described what happened? What was the formula which lay hidden in this mass of figures? What were the effects of a spherical implosion passing through a lump of plutonium the size of a small football? How could they come up with 'a workable formula for the propagation of a spherical detonation wave in a compressible fluid'? Under a pressure more intense than that at the earth's centre, the plutonium would reach 50,000,000°C in microseconds, becoming a 'compressible fluid'. The Nobel prizewinners past and future racked their brains over the figures. In the evenings Feynman, the brilliant probability theorist, and the great games theorist von Neumann, would relax at the poker school – and lose, just like the other geniuses, to the draft-dodging lab technician in Las Vegas shades. When the strain began clogging their minds, Feynman and von Neumann would take a walk through what was left of the local canyons, trying to talk their way around their theoretical problems – looking at them from some apparently insignificant angle which might prove fruitful. They had both noticed that when a shock wave passed through material it left certain squiggles of pressure in its wake that somehow couldn't be predicted. Feynman put this down to errors in his calculations, but von Neumann remained convinced that this couldn't be the case. Between the two of them, in casual conversation, they were elaborating the first outlines of chaos theory.

Eventually they worked out how to ensure

that the implosion method produced an even detonation. The explosive was arranged around the fissionable material in wedges. These were arranged symmetrically, so as to concentrate the shock waves on the central core in a precise fashion.

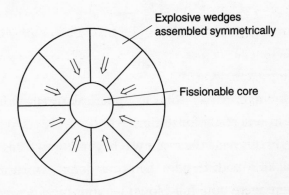

Explosive wedges
assembled symmetrically

Fissionable core

Each wedge would be detonated simultaneously. But to ensure maximum, evenly distributed pressure a mixture of fast and slow explosives would be used. This would 'focus' the shock waves on the surface of the fissionable material, so that their impact was evenly spread over the curved core.

The central part of the wave slows down as it passes through the slow explosive, ensuring that by the time the wave pattern reaches the central

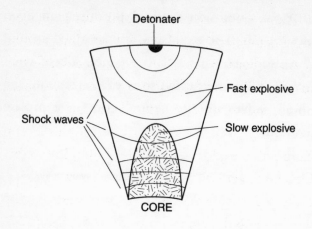

core it precisely 'fits' its spherical surface. Fat Man was ready for testing.

By this stage the strain was beginning to take its toll all round. Besides the prima donna tantrums, there were now full-blown nervous breakdowns. Even ice-cool Oppie was stretched to breaking-point. During the first months of 1945, while the 'gadget' was finally being assembled, he lost weight dramatically. Although over six feet tall, he soon only weighed just over eight stone! These were merely the physical manifestations: the mental effects have to be imagined. Oppie insisted on keeping such things to himself. He continued coolly chain-smoking – no matter how the excluded Kitty shrieked and smashed glasses.

The world's first atomic bomb was scheduled to be detonated 120 miles south of Albuquerque at Alamogordo in the New Mexico desert – the so-called 'Trinity Site'. It was to be a plutonium bomb, and it would be detonated atop a 100-foot steel tower. 10,000 yards (9 kms) from this 'Point Zero', the explosion would be monitored by Oppenheimer and his assembled experts from a protected bunker. VIPs and less essential staff would view the show from the Base Camp, 20 miles away.

Calculations of the effect of the blast differed, but Szilard had estimated that it would be in the region of 5,000 tons of TNT, and this was generally accepted. Everybody was worried about the effect of radioactive fallout, but no one really knew for certain how to predict its intensity or effect. And these weren't the only unpredictables. All were aware that they were launching into the unknown.

In the early hours of July 6th 1945, Oppenheimer and his team assembled in the bunker. The tall crow-like figure of Oppenheimer smoked incessantly, gulping down black coffee, as his team went through the final preparations.

Amidst the chill silence of the pre-dawn dark, the countdown finally reached zero at 5.30am.

The darkness of the last hour of night was suddenly rent by an intense blinding flash. This was followed by an eerily silent blast of heat. Moments later the heart-stopping roar of the shock wave tore over the bunker, echoing and re-echoing over the desert valley as the earth skipped and rumbled with its power. The faces in the bunker watched in awe as a vast molten fireball emerged from the horizon, more brilliant than the sun, casting its orange light over the desert floor as it rose into the sky. A huge mushroom cloud formed, gradually rising 40,000 feet into the upper atmosphere. His gaunt face aghast, Oppenheimer was aware of words from the *Bhagavad-Gita* rising into his mind:

'I am become Death,
The destroyer of worlds.'

Back at the Base Camp, Fermi had carried out a small private experiment. As the shock waves passed over the camp, having already crossed 20 miles of desert, Fermi surreptitiously let drop the piece of paper in his hand. Judging from the distance it was displaced, he reckoned the blast had been the equivalent of 20,000 tons of TNT. This was four times Szilard's estimate – but when they checked the instruments it was found that Fermi's little experiment had proved right. The 100-foot steel tower at Point Zero had simply vaporized, and the intense heat had scorched the desert sand for a radius of 800 yards into a sheet of glass. The world had entered the Nuclear Age.

But what was to be the immediate effect of this new weapon, which for the first time gave humanity the power to put an end to itself? The news of Germany's surrender had arrived at the Trinity Site *prior* to the test detonation – just as the final preliminary explosives trials were being carried out. At last the race with the Germans was over! Surely there was no need to continue with the test now?

But Oppenheimer was informed that nothing would be changed. The president changed (Roosevelt died and was succeeded by Truman), the target changed (becoming Japan, instead of Germany) – but nothing changed.

It had ever been thus. Right from the start, the

Manhattan Project had proved unstoppable. Not long after his arrival in the United States, Bohr had begun to experience misgivings about atomic weapons. In 1944 he had written to Roosevelt, urging him to share the secret of nuclear fission with the allies (including the Russians), so that an international agreement could be reached on the control of such weapons. But feelings on this topic ran high. When Churchill got wind of Bohr's proposal, he declared that he should be flung in jail at once. Early in 1945 Szilard sent Roosevelt a petition, signed by a list of eminent scientists, calling for international control of atomic weapons. He stated prophetically: 'the greatest immediate danger . . . is the probability that our "demonstration" of atomic bombs will precipitate a race in the production of such devices between the United States and Russia.'

Oppenheimer did not sign Szilard's petition. He had his misgivings, but he kept them largely to himself – or spoke of them in gnomic terms. 'Physicists have known sin,' he remarked after the Trinity test. Later, he 'rationalized' his position: 'I set forth my anxieties and the arguments against dropping [the bomb], but I did not endorse them.' To Truman, he finally confessed: 'Mr President, I feel I have blood on my hands.' Truman merely pulled out his handkerchief, and said: 'Would you like to wipe them?' (Although he'd been vice-president, Truman himself had remained blissfully ignorant of the Manhattan Project until he succeeded to the presidency, weeks before the Trinity test.)

When Truman arrived at Potsdam for the allied conference which followed victory in Germany, he informed Stalin that the Americans had a new super-weapon. Proudly he announced that this had just been successfully tested in the New Mexico desert. Truman was puzzled at Stalin's lack of surprise. He needn't have been – Stalin had known about the Manhattan Project years before he had! Stalin's sole response to the news of the bomb was that he hoped the Americans would make 'good use of it against the Japanese'.

And this is precisely what happened. Under the tightest security, aimed at excluding all Russian spies (who weren't already operating on the inside), the US military set about complying with Stalin's wishes – just as he already knew they would. (For some months now, Klaus Fuchs had been joined at Los Alamos by the brother of the Rosenbergs, who were to become the most famous Russian spies of them all.)

At 9.14am on 6th August 1945, a single US B-29 bomber dropped a uranium-filled Little Boy atomic bomb on Hiroshima. In an instant, 4 square miles of the city were flattened, 66,000 were killed and 69,000 were wounded. (Lingering effects would more than double these casualty figures over the years.) Three days later a plutonium-filled Fat Man atomic bomb was dropped on Nagasaki, and the Japanese surrendered the following day.

Despite this atomic carnage, the Japanese surrender certainly saved countless thousands of lives, both Japanese and American. The Japanese had been ordered to fight to the last man, and at Iwo Jima they had shown they were willing to do exactly that. However, one salient fact is often overlooked: precisely five months before Hiroshima, an American B-29 bombing raid on Tokyo had killed 83,000 (ie, 17,000 more than initially at Hiroshima) and left 1½ million homeless. Should the Americans have persisted with such conventional bombing, instead of resorting to nuclear weapons? If the Japanese had not surrendered after a raid which laid waste so much of their capital city, when would they? Historians continue to argue the pros and cons of the start of nuclear warfare – the scourge which could yet ensure that the pioneers of evolution on this planet, for the next million years, are a few species of radioactive-resistant dung-beetle.

In October 1945 Oppenheimer resigned from Los Alamos, so that he could return to academic life. In his resignation speech to the assembled geniuses and 'intelligence', he stated baldly: 'If atomic bombs are added to the arsenals of a warring world . . . mankind will curse the name of Los Alamos.'

Oppenheimer returned to Caltech. But he knew that he would never be able to escape from what he had done – even if he wanted to. (Oppenheimer was to remain ambivalent on this point: he was always *proud* of being the 'father of the bomb', despite his growing misgivings about the bomb itself.) In 1947 he accepted the post of Chairman of the General Advisory Committee of the Atomic Energy Commission.

In the same year he took over as head of the Institute for Advanced Study, now indisputably the finest theoretical research centre in the world. Here he presided over the likes of Einstein, Gödel and von Neumann – the gods of the mathematical universe. Oppenheimer knew, and enjoyed, such company; but he was not at all impressed with the way the IAS functioned. It was 'a madhouse; its solipsistic luminaries shining in separate and helpless desolation'. Gödel, having destroyed mathematics, now appeared to be doing the same to himself (he did eventually starve himself to death). And even the sophisticated von Neumann had become so absent-minded that on one occasion, when he was driving to New York, he had to ring home and ask his wife why he was going there. Oppenheimer agreed with Einstein that so many old men were turning 'the Institute into an institution'.

Oppenheimer began bringing in younger men, who stayed for shorter periods. He also thought there were too many mathematicians in residence, and sought to redress the balance in favour of physicists. By the very nature of things, even theoretical physicists tended to have more contact with the world around them, and here he led by example. Living at the IAS in Princeton meant that Oppenheimer could now cultivate his contacts in Washington. Here he was regarded as something of an *eminence grise*, and was increasingly consulted on scientific matters by the powers that be, as well as visiting foreign statesmen. Oppenheimer enjoyed his new-found status, though it didn't help his natural inclination to arrogance.

The world was now entering the most frigid period of the Cold War, with American troops fighting the communists in Korea and the Russians announcing that they too now had an atomic bomb. Despite this, Oppenheimer's committee advised the Atomic Energy Commission against America developing a hydrogen bomb (conservatively predicted to be hundreds of times more powerful than an atomic bomb). This decision was not well-received, and was quickly overruled by the AEC chairman, Rear-Admiral Lewis L Strauss. These were difficult times. The Rosenbergs had just been arrested for selling atomic secrets to the Russians, and Senator

McCarthy had begun his notorious anti-communist 'witch-hunts', which were to wreck countless innocent careers.

The McCarthy era was under way. Yet despite Oppenheimer's difficulties with the security services and the FBI, he felt quite safe. After all, he had played a major role in helping America win the war. And he now had friends in very high places indeed. But as he rose, so did his nose. Oppenheimer was becoming a very superior person. He'd never tolerated fools gladly, and he saw no reason to change now. Especially if that fool was the gung-ho chairman of the Atomic Energy Commission, and was opposed to the more sophisticated, less confrontational approach advocated by the chairman of its Advisory Committee.

There was no hiding the fact: former Rear Admiral Lewis L Strauss couldn't stand 'intellectual Oppie'. Strauss had started life as a door-to-door shoe salesman in the mining region of West Virginia. He may never have been to college, but when he went to New York he quickly worked out how to operate on Wall Street. By the outbreak of the war he was a multi-millionaire. This helped him to a commission in the navy, where he rose to rear admiral and subsequent power in Washington. Strauss had one basic policy: if you didn't agree with him, you were out. The H-bomb was to be *his* baby, and after Oppenheimer's opposition Strauss ordered him to be investigated. The director of the world's most prestigious theoretical research institute, the nuclear physicist who had masterminded the technical achievement which won America the war, once again had his phone tapped, his mail opened, his every move shadowed by flatfoots in wide-brimmed hats.

Oppenheimer regarded such treatment with the contempt it deserved. But alas, Oppenheimer was far too skilled at contempt for his own good. In 1953, when he was called to give evidence before the Atomic Energy Commission in a public hearing, he couldn't resist having a dig at its chairman. Under questioning, Oppenheimer coolly proceeded to expose the committee's ignorance of nuclear science, at the same time exposing its chairman's anti-communist paranoia. When the committee demanded to know the defensive importance of isotopes, Oppenheimer explained sarcastically that they were 'far more important than, let us say, vitamins'.

There were a few sniggers from the public, and Strauss scowled.

But they could be used to make atomic energy, persisted the committee.

Oppenheimer agreed, but added: 'You can use a shovel for atomic energy. In fact you do.'

Roars of laughter, Strauss like thunder.

'You can use a bottle of beer for atomic energy,' persisted Oppenheimer.

In an attempt to defuse the situation, another member of the committee asked Oppenheimer what was the best security.

'The best security is the grave,' remarked Oppenheimer.

Afterwards, one of Strauss's loyal colleagues announced: 'More probably than not J Robert Oppenheimer is an agent of the Soviet Union.'

This should of course have been laughable – but humour was in short supply in the political circles of 1950s Washington. (It took the general public to realize that McCarthy was a joke. When he appeared on TV and exposed himself as the drunken demagogue he was, his influence dwindled almost overnight.)

Strauss was now determined to get mister smarty-pants Oppenheimer. In 1954 Oppenheimer was hauled before a security hearing. He was accused of 'associating with known communists' (his brother), and opposing the development of the hydrogen bomb (his job). No one laughed. But with such charges it was difficult to pin anything serious on Oppenheimer. Reluctantly, the committee was forced to declare that Oppenheimer was not guilty of treason. (For which the Rosenbergs had just been sent to the electric chair.) Instead, in a vindictive gesture, his security clearance was withdrawn.

This meant Oppenheimer was forbidden all access to classified documents and sacked from his government posts. Once sought out by top officials and visiting dignitaries, he was suddenly a pariah in Washington.

The high life was over for J Robert Oppenheimer, and he slunk home to the IAS a humiliated man. His treatment over the next few months broke him. Strauss, of all people, had been appointed a trustee of the Institute for Advanced Study – and now did his best to make

Oppenheimer's life hell. His office was bugged (again), his mail (including incoming academic material) was scrutinised and censored (presumably by the advanced nuclear physics department of the FBI). And Oppenheimer was even barred from his director's office while his personal safe was chiselled from the wall and removed, so that all classified documents contained in it could be recovered. But he wasn't sacked from being director of the IAS – Einstein, Gödel, von Neumann et al signed a forcibly worded statement which saw to that.

Oppenheimer quickly became an international symbol: though of what, isn't quite clear. As always with Oppenheimer, the situation was complex. He had made his Faustian pact with the devil – he'd created the bomb. And his incorrigibly ambivalent attitude towards this achievement meant that he was no moral hero. Unlike Bohr, the great chemist Linus Pauling, or the philosopher Bertrand Russell, all of whom went further than Oppenheimer's somewhat hesitant suggestion of international control for atomic weapons, Oppenheimer was in it up to his neck. It was his baby, and in the end he really didn't know what to do with it. So what exactly *was* he a symbol of? If anything, all this makes Oppenheimer very much an emblem of the scientist today. Technically supreme, yet morally uncertain. The possibility of nuclear disaster has now been joined by the more insidious possibility of ecological disaster. With Oppenheimer, science changed: the great creator also became the great destroyer. Science has now taken over as humanity's foremost endeavour – yet Oppenheimer's conflict between pride and morality continues. And even widens.

In the months following his security hearing, Oppenheimer's appearance changed drastically. His hair turned grey, once again he became skeletally thin, and he developed a number of trembles and tics. Always a heavy drinker, he now chose to join Kitty in her long alcoholic evenings. Yet surprisingly, he remained an excellent director of the IAS. Administration of genius was ever his forte.

Not for nine years was justice done. In November 1963 President Kennedy belatedly decided to name Oppenheimer for the prestigious Enrico Fermi Award. This was to be

Oppenheimer's public pardon; but on the very day Kennedy made his decision he was assassinated. President Johnson, however, honoured this commitment; the picture of the award ceremony shows Johnson beaming down at a wizened bespectacled old man. Yet despite this public pardon, Oppenheimer was never given back his security clearance. Less than four years later, early in 1967, Oppenheimer died of throat cancer at the age of 62.

SOME FACTS & FIZZLES ON THE BOMB

• The 'argument' for the nuclear deterrent unintentionally exposed in all its absurdity:

'We will not act prematurely or unnecessarily risk the costs of world-wide nuclear war in which even the fruits of victory would be ashes in our mouth. But neither will we shrink from that risk at any time it must be faced.'

John F. Kennedy

'No country without an atom bomb could properly consider itself independent.'

Charles de Gaulle

'It isn't important to come out on top, what matters is to be the one who comes out alive.'

Bertolt Brecht

• The atom bomb in a nutshell: two subcritical masses of fissionable material (such as Uranium

235) are brought together to form a critical mass. This causes an uncontrollable chain reaction, resulting in a nuclear explosion of around 20 kilotons.

• 1 kiloton = explosive power of 1,000 tons of TNT
  1 megaton = explosive power of 1,000,000 tons of TNT
  On detonation TNT (trinitrotoluene) generates a pressure of around 270,000 atmospheres (4,000,000 pounds per square inch).

• A hydrogen bomb releases an explosion in the megaton range. This is a thermo-nuclear weapon which typically uses a fission-fusion device. It usually consists of a fission bomb surrounded by heavy hydrogen. The detonated fission device causes fusion in the surrounding heavy hydrogen.

• In fission, the bombarding neutron divides the nucleus, releasing a vast amount of energy.

In fusion, two nuclei are brought together with such force that they fuse, a process which results in an even vaster release of energy.

'If the human race wants to go to hell in a basket, technology can help it get there by jet. It won't change the desire or the direction, but it can greatly speed the passage.'

Charles M. Allen

'Man has wrested from nature the power to make the world a desert or the deserts bloom. There is no evil in the atom; only in men's souls.'

Adlai Stevenson

'I don't know what will be the most important weapon in the next war, but I know what will be the most important weapon in the war after that – the bow and arrow.'

Anon

• A neutron bomb is a thermo-nuclear device which also uses the fission–fusion method. It produces a limited blast, but scatters vast amounts of lethal gamma and neutron radiation over a large area. This can penetrate almost all known armour-plating, and is lethal to human life. Such bombs would be useful for eliminating an army without destroying its weapons, or turning cities into instant museums for space visitors.

'A weapon is an enemy, even to its owner.'

Turkish saying

'The only way to survive the bomb is not to be around when it goes off.'

CND leaflet

During war 'the latest refinements of science are linked with the cruelties of the Stone Age'.

Winston Churchill

• Nuclear energy is obtained from nuclear fission or fusion. The chain reaction is slowed down, and thus 'controlled'.

Uranium produces around 2,500,000 times more energy than the same weight of coal.

The fusion process, using heavy hydrogen, produces another 400 times more than that.

'The unleashed power of the atom has changed everything save our modes of thinking and we thus drift toward unparalleled catastrophe.'

Albert Einstein

THE HISTORY OF
THE BOMB

1789   Klaproth discovers uranium

1900   The electron discovered by Thomson

1905   Einstein publishes Special Theory of
        Relativity, which later gives rise to
        formula $e = mc^2$

1931   The atom first split by Cockroft and
        Walton at Cavendish Laboratory in
        Cambridge

1934   Joliot-Curies bombard atomic nuclei
        with alpha particles – producing new
        elements. The discovery of artificial
        radioactivity

1934   Enrico Fermi bombards atomic nuclei
        with neutrons, but is unaware of full
        import of his experiments

1938   Hahn and Meitner continue Fermi's
        work, bombarding uranium with
        neutrons

1939   Meitner interprets results of her experiments with Hahn, realising that nucleus has been split in two. She names this process 'nuclear fission'

1939   After hearing from Bohr, Einstein and Szilard contact President Roosevelt, warning him of the dangers of Germany using nuclear fission in a bomb. Manhattan Project initiated

1942   Fermi builds world's first nuclear reactor in Chicago, and produces first controlled chain reaction

1942   Los Alamos set up in New Mexico

1945   First atomic bomb detonated at Trinity Site in New Mexico. A month later atomic bombs dropped on Hiroshima and Nagasaki

1952   America tests first hydrogen bomb at Eniwetok Atol in the Pacific

1953   Russia tests hydrogen bomb

1957   Britain tests hydrogen bomb

1967   China tests hydrogen bomb

1968   France tests hydrogen bomb

1970s   America develops neutron bomb

1980s   India, Israel, and Brazil develop
          nuclear weapons
1990s   Pakistan, North Korea and Iraq
          developing nuclear weapons. France
          persists in testing nuclear bombs in
          Pacific

SUGGESTIONS FOR FURTHER READING

Peter Goodchild: *J Robert Oppenheimer*, (BBC) – Serviceable full-length biography, with large number of excellent photos.

Richard Rhodes: *The Making of the Atomic Bomb*, (Simon & Schuster) – Emphasis on relations between government and science in the Manhattan Project: intricate and fascinating.

Jack Rummell: *Robert Oppenheimer*, (Facts on File) – Shorter biography with good coverage of scientific development of the bomb.

Robert Oppenheimer: *Science and the Common Understanding* – Clear exposition of modern physics, especially quantum mechanics, from the maestro himself. An absolute minimum of jargon renders this comprehensible to all.